FIFTY
CHAIRS
THAT
CHANGED
THE
WORLD

DESIGN MUSEUM

FIFTY CHAIRS THAT CHANGED THE WORLD

conran OCTOPUS

FIFTY CHAIRS

FIFTY CHAIRS

It would be possible to trace the history of design in the past 150 years simply through a sequence of chairs. At the very beginning the story would trace the work of the Austrian company Thonet, whose transformation of furniture-making into an industrial process through the abolition of craft skills could be taken as representing the impact of mass production on design of all kinds. The use of tubular steel by Marcel Breuer had a similar impact and significance, as did Charles and Ray Eames's work with plastics.

The iconic, representative role played by the chair has been something of a self-fulfilling prophecy. Because chairs have become such important markers of stylistic and technological shifts, architects and designers who want to be considered important have to have designed at least one successful example to demonstrate their credentials. A chair is itself but it is also so much more.

Chairs have a long history – so long that the word has become deeply embedded into language. We have chairmen and chairwomen, seats of power, ex cathedra ('from the chair') pronouncements ... and so on. Chairs can symbolize authority, identity and domesticity. And because they provide such a restricted canvas, they give their designers very little room to hide – a chair is a poem, rather than a novel.

For all these reasons, the Design Museum values its collection of contemporary chairs, and this book provides an introduction to 50 of the key chairs that have shaped the story of design.

Deyan Sudjic, Director, Design Museum

Right: Alvar Aalto's stacking stools Model No. 60 laid out in rows in the Lecture Room of the Viipuri Public Library (1933–5), During the twentieth century many Modernist designers and architects made chairs for specific contexts.

SIDE CHAIR NO.14

1859
Thonet

The gestural twists and compressed arcs of the Thonet Side chair No.14 evoke the timeless romance of a pavement café. They give little away, however, about the revolution in modern mass manufacture that this unobtrusive and overfamiliar piece of furniture represents.

Until the late nineteenth century, chairs were by and large handmade. However, evolving demand provoked manufacturers to develop methods of mass manufacture that relied on new technologies and embraced new commercial markets. By 1859 the Austrian-based furniture manufacturer Thonet – founded by Michael Thonet (1796–1871) in the 1830s – had successfully developed a chair made of just six pieces of steam-bent wood, ten screws and two washers. Cheap and fast to make, lightweight and durable, easy to disassemble and transport, Side chair No.14 – often known by its German nickname, the *Konsumstuhl* – rapidly became one of the most successful industrial products of the nineteenth century.

Of chair No.14 Le Corbusier is said to have stated, 'Never was a better and more elegant design and a more precisely crafted and practical item ever created.' The chair has remained synonymous with relaxed café culture. Variations of the shape are still made today, though often out of materials – such as welded metal – that have little to do with the original conception of what was perhaps the first piece of flatpack furniture.

Right: An ubiquitous addition to cafés, bars and public spaces, the Thonet Side chair is probably one of the most recognizable, most produced, and most reinterpreted chairs of all time. Below: The chair is made out of a series of mass-produced bentwood components that are then screwed together.

HIGH-BACKED CHAIR FOR MISS CRANSTON'S TEA ROOMS

1900
Charles Rennie
Mackintosh

The turn of the twentieth century brought with it a wave of groundbreaking designers and architects who helped pioneer the Modern movement. In Scotland, Charles Rennie Mackintosh (1868–1928) eloquently fused traditional Celtic craftsmanship with fashionable *japoniste* rigour, to create a distinctive style suspended between Art Nouveau, Arts and Crafts, and Central European Secessionism. Mackintosh's work – often carried out in collaboration with his wife, Margaret MacDonald (1865–1933) – spanned the disciplines of architecture, decorative painting and furniture to produce experiential interiors of startling modernity – the design equivalent of the Wagnerian *Gesamtkunstwerk*, or 'total artwork'.

In 1900 Catherine Cranston commissioned Mackintosh to design a ladies' lunch room for her extensive Tea Rooms at 205 Ingram Street, at the heart of Glasgow's mercantile district. Mackintosh's finished interior was at once austere and luxurious – the full-height windows and high wood panelling insistently emphasizing the dramatic verticality of his design. The severe geometric form of the high-backed chair, positioned along the tea tables in near-military rows, continued the theme, and was softened only by such decorative detailing as the play of arced forms found in the pierced headrest, upholstery and panel between the back legs.

Mackintosh's elegant architectural compositions would have a far-reaching influence on the development of early twentieth-century European design – most notably, perhaps, on the work of the Austrian Josef Hoffmann and other designers associated with the Wiener Werkstätte (see pages 12–17). The simple, forthright high-backed chairs themselves – of which Mackintosh produced many variations – have remained a classic.

Right: The elongated, geometrically influenced shape of Charles Rennie Mackintosh's chair for Miss Cranston's Tea Rooms was at the forefront of developing a new visual language for twentieth-century design.

ARMCHAIR FOR THE PURKERSDORF SANATORIUM

1904–5
Koloman Moser

This radically geometric chair typifies the work of the Wiener Werkstätte, the influential 'Viennese craft workshops' founded in 1903 by a group of avant-garde designers associated with the Vienna Secession – notably the graphic designer Koloman Moser (1868–1918) and the architect Josef Hoffmann (1870–1956).

The founders of the Wiener Werkstätte took their inspiration from C R Ashbee's Guild of Handicraft set up in London's East End in 1888. An exhibition of British-crafted objects in Vienna in 1900, and visits to the city by notable British designers including Ashbee and Charles Rennie Mackintosh (see pages 10–11), helped ensure British influence among the Viennese design community. Like the Guild, the Wiener Werkstätte valued both good forward-thinking design and high-quality traditional craftsmanship.

Like Mackintosh's high-backed chair, Moser's armchair was designed as part of a coordinated project, linking architecture and interior design. The Purkersdorf Sanatorium (1904–5), designed by Hoffmann, was the Wiener Werkstätte's first major commission, in which the designers took responsibility for everything from the iron-and-concrete building itself to every last detail of the interior. Moser's armchairs stood in the sanatorium foyer, arranged neatly around tall octagonal tables. The boxlike structure and checked seating replicated the 'square' theme found on the walls and the floor and created an atmosphere of luxurious modernity for what was essentially a fashionable hotel and health farm.

Right: With its rhythmically repetitive cage-like structure and chequered seat, Moser's armchair for the Purkersdorf Sanatorium heralds an aesthetic for the modern age.

SITZMASCHINE

c.1905
Josef Hoffmann

In the earliest years of the twentieth century, designers were not only challenging preconceptions about how things should look but also exploring the ways in which design impacted on people's lives. The world was changing rapidly and very visibly. New 'column-frame' construction techniques were thrusting buildings high into the sky, while early motor vehicles were intruding noisily into the urban street scene. The aptly named Sitzmaschine ('machine for sitting') – one of Josef Hoffmann's innovations created for the luxurious health spa at Purkersdorf (see pages 12–13) – is an important example of how mechanization was filtering into design as a major new theme.

While the Sitzmaschine is undeniably a descendant of the Arts and Crafts Morris chair designed by Philip Webb (1831–1915) in 1866, in its rationalized form and construction this was a chair that had its sights set firmly on the Machine Age. With its streamlined form made up of sweeping bent-beechwood curves and sycamore panels pierced with geometric grids of square and rectangular apertures, the Sitzmaschine's aesthetic echoes the moving components of a belt-driven engine.

The chair has mechanized functions of its own, too – the backrest tilts and is then secured with a rod that rests on one of a succession of pairs of spherical knobs. For all its vaunted utilitarian functionality, however, the Sitzmaschine is, above all, an elegant exercise in geometric abstraction.

Right: Even the name of Josef Hoffman's Sitzmaschine seems to inaugurate a new, functionalist approach to chair design.

CHAIR NO. 728 FOR THE CABARET FLEDERMAUS

In 1907 the Wiener Werkstätte completed another ambitious project – the design for the Cabaret Fledermaus at 22 Kärtner Straße, Vienna – which encompassed not only the interior decor but also the furnishings, tableware and even the badge worn by the usherettes. Involved in the collaboration were such illustrious names as Gustav Klimt and Oskar Kokoschka and, of course, the Werkstätte's *genius loci*, Josef Hoffmann.

Hoffmann's most remarkable contribution was undoubtedly this simple, clean-cut chair, which was arranged around the similarly restrained round tables, also Hoffmann-designed. The design's modesty and lack of ostentation was the perfect foil for the Jugendstil splendour of the rest of the decor, most notably the exuberant 7,000-piece majolica mosaic by Bertold Löffler and Michael Polwony.

A critic of the time described the whole effect of the Cabaret Fledermaus in glowing terms: '[it is] wonderful – the proportions, the light atmosphere, cheerful flowing lines, elegant light fixtures, comfortable chairs of new shape and, finally, the whole tasteful ensemble. Genuine Hoffmann.'

Right: Josef Hoffmann's clean-cut chair pictured in the meticulously designed interior for which it was made. Below: The minimalist structure of the Cabaret Fledermaus chair made it radically modern. Only the small black spheres beneath the armrests and seat add a faint note of whimsy.

RED/BLUE CHAIR

The Red/Blue chair designed by the architect Gerrit Thomas Rietveld (1888–1964) was at the forefront of the experiments undertaken by different members of the Dutch-based De Stijl movement. Founded in 1917, the group sought to instil Neoplatonic thought into design, creating ultimate objects that expressed the perfection and spiritual harmony of geometry and primary colour.

The Red/Blue chair was among the first experiments to apply the De Stijl philosophy to 3D form and is a rigorous construction of straight lines and flat planes of primary colour; three-dimensional form has been turned into an elemental expression of pure abstraction. The chair was originally painted in the typical De Stijl palette of grey, black and white, but in 1918 Reitveld repainted it in red, blue, yellow and black to echo the paintings of fellow De Stijl member Piet Mondrian (1872–1944).

The startling aesthetic of this piece of furniture caused a sensation, and – as with Mondrian's gridlike paintings – the chair has continued to evoke the look of abstract modernity up to the present day. While Rietveld had originally intended the chair for mass production (it was made out of standard lengths of wood that required little skill to construct), this never, in fact, occurred. Today the Red/Blue chair remains an iconic one-off – as a realized idea of a chair – in the Toledo Museum of Art in Ohio.

Right: Gerrit Thomas Reitveld's sculptural and brightly coloured chair abandoned traditional styles and motifs in favour of pure abstraction as the way forward for modern design.

B3 – LATER KNOWN AS THE WASSILY CHAIR

1925
Marcel Breuer

The Model B3 was one of the earliest products to emerge from the Dessau Bauhaus and helped consolidate the school's reputation as the leading force in functional design. It was one of the earliest designs, too, to exploit tubular steel, whose structural strength, lightness and stark, sleek looks enabled the creation of striking new furniture forms.

Its designer, Marcel Breuer (1902–81) – the head of the Bauhaus cabinet-making workshop – is said to have taken some of his inspiration from the tubular-steel handlebars of his beloved Adler bicycle. Breuer gave one of the earliest prototypes to his Bauhaus colleague, the painter Wassily Kandinsky, after whom the chair was eventually to be renamed when it was reissued in the 1960s. The chair was initially manufactured by the pioneering Austrian furniture company Thonet (see pages 8–9) and was available in black, white or wire-mesh fabric, and in both folding and non-folding forms.

The Model B3 was a solution to the technical challenge of redefining what a chair should look like and how it should be made. While its refined structure, outlined by thin nickel-plated pipes of metal, make it look rather like a technical line drawing, in fact its broad volume and simple styling produce the perfect chair.

Right: Built from the same material as his beloved Alder bicycle, Marcel Breuer's B3 chair is one of the first examples of tubular-steel technology filtering into furniture design.

CANTILEVER

Marcel Breuer was not the only designer experimenting with tubular-steel furniture. In 1925 the Dutch architect Mart Stam (1899–1996) – at the time resident in Berlin – developed a chair without any back legs that relied instead – in appearance at least – on the strength of a single twisting piece of piping to support and counterbalance the weight of a seated person.

Stam's design was perhaps – the matter is open to dispute – the first manifestation of the cantilever chair – an innovation that was to have a massive impact on the course of furniture design in the mid twentieth century. Stam's design was rigid and somewhat uncomfortable, however, and it would be left to other furniture designers to develop the 'bounce' that would make the experience of perching on such a chair feel like sitting on, as Breuer put it on, 'an elastic pillar of air'.

Such developments were swiftly adopted by contemporaries such as Breuer (see pages 26–7) and Mies van der Rohe and rival adaptations were patented within the same year. This led to legal wrangling between Stam and Breuer in the German courts to determine to whom the copyright should be attributed. Stam eventually won, but this bitter struggle demonstrates just how vital the cantilevered breakthrough must have seemed to pioneering designers at the time.

Right: Sleek, simple … and revolutionary. Mart Stam created his experimental cantilever chair out of commercial gas pipes and joint fittings. His pioneering work was very rapidly taken up by other avant-garde designers and was to have an enormous impact on mid twentieth-century design.

TRANSAT

With its exactness of finish and diagrammatic composition of structure and form, the Transat chair is an important precursor of the aesthetic of mass manufacture and mechanical process. Its deckchair format evokes the luxurious ease of transatlantic travel, from which it took its name.

For many years the Irish designer and architect Eileen Gray (1878–1976) has been a forgotten pioneer of the Modern movement, overshadowed by more heralded contemporaries such as Le Corbusier (1887–1965) and Robert Mallet-Stevens (1886–1945). She was a rare woman in a world dominated by male designers and architects, and was all the more isolated because, unlike many other women designers who made an impact on early twentieth-century design, she did not work alongside a male collaborator.

Of independent means, Gray was able to finance her own education and creative pursuits, switching disciplines as her interests evolved. Initially she studied painting at the Slade School of Fine Art in London, but she turned to design after becoming absorbed in the painstaking craft of lacquerwork. Largely basing herself in Paris, she gradually won both commercial and critical acclaim, leading to ever larger commissions that eventually included whole interiors.

The Transat became one of Gray's signature pieces – one in which she combined her knowledge of intricately worked and finished wood with a geometric framework that would now be more closely associated with extruded and welded steel. Gray's search for innovation and perfection of form ranks her as a visionary who helped redefine how things should look and be made in the Machine Age.

Right: Eileen Gray created the Transat chair for House E-1027 – the holiday home near Monaco she shared and co-designed with her lover, the Romanian architect Jean Badovici. The chair's sleek, luxurious form evokes the sun-drenched pleasures of ocean-going travel.

B32

Following on from Mart Stam's work (see pages 22–3) Marcel Breuer's own researches into the cantilever chair found its most perfect resolution in the Model B32 – widely considered to be the most refined of all the pioneering cantilevered designs that emerged in the late 1920s. Another fruit of Breuer's Bauhaus cabinet-making workshop (see pages 20–1), this chair has survived the test of time, regaining popularity after being reissued in the 1960s and 1970s.

By adding wooden frames to act as seat and backrest, Breuer cleverly removed the need for the additional supports and hidden tubes that had been present in earlier versions, including Stam's. This made for a simplified lightweight structure that combined the warmth and transparency of woven cane with the harsher aesthetics of the industrial metal frame.

Breuer also experimented with variations – the B64 added armrests to create a striking armchair version of the B32.

Right: With its slick and slender tubular metal and traditional woven-wicker seat and backrest, the B32 has sat comfortably in modern interiors from the 1920s to the present day. Below: Marcel Breuer's cantilever chair is an instantly recognizable classic of twentieth-century design.

BARCELONA

The Barcelona chair remains the ubiquitous choice for anonymous corporate office foyers across the globe. Its origins, however, are altogether more illustrious.

In 1929 the German architect Ludwig Mies van der Rohe (1886–1969) collaborated with his compatriot, the interior designer Lilly Reich (1885–1947), on the German Pavilion at the 1929 Ibero-American Exposition in Barcelona. The pavilion was to be used for the exhibition's opening ceremony and accordingly neither expense nor effort was spared. Marble, travertine, brass and plate glass were deployed to majestic effect, and within the cool, calm interior the Barcelona chairs and accompanying ottomans took on a monumental presence.

The chairs were luxurious and sleekly modern, combining reflective chrome with ivory pigskin leather (later versions usually used black bovine leather instead). Low, broad and slightly tilted, the chair managed to suggest both comfort and formality, luxury and spareness. Unlike many other Modernist designers, who at least claimed to be designing affordable products, Mies van der Rohe unabashedly aimed for the high end of the market.

The Barcelona chair went into commercial production only in 1953 when Mies van der Rohe sold the rights to Knoll, and it continues to be manufactured by that US company today. The chair currently sells at upwards of $4,000, though unlicensed replicas are commonplace. Those in search of the real thing might like to make the pilgrimage to Barcelona, where the German Pavilion, complete with the iconic chairs, was rebuilt in the 1980s.

Right: Barcelona chairs in the interior of the German Pavilion, designed by Ludwig Mies van der Rohe and Lilly Reich for the 1929 Ibero-American Exhibition in Barcelona. In the foreground are examples of the accompanying Barcelona ottoman. Below: The chair has become a classic – some might add, hackneyed – statement of modernity in corporate buildings across the world.

PAIMIO LOUNGE CHAIR

1930–1
Alvar Aalto

As the twentieth century progressed, new technologies and ideologies were combined as designers challenged the past and sought to shape a different, and better, future. They were still far from finding mass-market approval, however, and one stratagem that many architects and designers adopted was to use commissions for municipal projects such as hospitals and schools to develop and manufacture new radical work.

One who did so was the Finnish architect Alvar Aalto (1898–1976) who, in the late 1920s, designed the building, fixtures and fittings for the Paimio Sanatorium (completed 1932), a tuberculosis hospital in western Finland. Aalto approached the commission with a deep sense of empathy for the sanatorium's future patients and was insistent that every aspect should contribute to the healing process. This included the meticulous planning of the building's layout, a bright and cheering choice of paint to adorn the walls, and robust, comfortable furniture. The whole hospital, he said, was to be a 'medical instrument'.

The sanatorium had large sun terraces where patients were encouraged to spend many hours as part of their treatment. The Paimio lounge chair was the climax of three years of experimentation to create a chair that would feel comfortable to sit in over long periods and help ease patients' breathing. The scroll-like seat was moulded from a single piece of birch plywood, while its flexing structure made the wood feel 'soft' and welcoming.

Right above: The Paimio lounge chair offered comfort and support to patients at the Finnish sanatorium. Right below: The chair also sits well within a modern domestic interior, pictured here with a stacking stool, Model No. 60, also by Alvar Aalto (see pages 32–3).

STACKING STOOL MODEL NO. 60

Alvar Aalto originally designed this simple, elegant stool for the Viipuri Library (now Vyborg, Russia) – a High Modernist building designed by Aalto in the early 1930s. While Aalto was profoundly influenced by the tubular-metal designs of contemporaries such as Marcel Breuer, he was determined to nurture his own distinctive style using traditional Finnish materials such as birch.

The stacking stool is unadorned and unassuming, but, owing to the colour and texture of the varnished wood, warm and welcoming nonetheless. When seen in serried groups – as in a well-known 1930s photograph of the auditorium with its wavelike wooden roof (see page 7) – the stool can appear clonelike, but as an individual piece it nevertheless manages to communicate a quirky personality with its squat proportions and curve-topped legs.

In 1933 Aalto exhibited the stool alongside his Paimio lounge chair at London's famed Fortnum & Mason department store, where it caused a sensation. These pieces of furniture were no longer just for the studious or convalescent. They now also represented aspirational modern living, as Modernism began to develop into a luxury international brand.

Right: When the Model No. 60 is stacked, the legs form a sculptural spiral. Below: This simple, sturdy and versatile piece of furniture has become a classic for public and private interiors.

ZIG-ZAG

1932–4
Gerrit Thomas Rietveld

Although Gerrit Thomas Rietveld broke with De Stijl in 1928, his Zig-Zag chair is another statement of abstraction that succinctly puts into practice the principles of the Dutch design movement. As with his Red/Blue chair of a decade and a half earlier (see pages 18–19), the Zig-Zag is a pared-down representation of form and colour that abandons any reference to natural form or tradition.

In essence, of course, the Zig-Zag is also yet another example of the cantilever chair that had so preoccupied the avant-garde in the previous decade. Here the problem is resolved in a series of sheer wooden planes – originally, oak – to create a strikingly sculptural form. The strong diagonal lines owe much to an acute understanding of structural engineering, but they are also said to have been a response to a call by Rietveld's former colleague, the De Stijl theorist Theo van Doesburg (1883–1931), for the introduction of oblique lines into interior design.

Right: An origami squiggle of a chair – the radical visual simplicity of Gerrit Thomas Rietveld's design belies the sophisticated understanding of structural principles that underlie it.

CHAIR NO. 406

At the time of its conception in the late 1930s, chair No. 406 would have seemed a miracle of gravity-defying design. With its S-shaped outline and thin birch frame, this elegant, cantilevered chair would have challenged most contemporary preconceptions of how timber – that most traditional of domestic design materials – could be used.

The 'miracle' was made possible by the tensile qualities of laminated wood, with which several designers were experimenting at this time. Before this period, innovation in furniture design had been dominated by experimentation with metal. Now designers such as Alvar Aalto in Finland, Marcel Breuer, then in England, and Bruno Mathsson (1907–88) in Sweden, were re-embracing and pushing the technical boundaries of wood to forge a new, more humanized Modernist aesthetic that is still familiar today.

While designing chair No. 406, Aalto was also working on the Finnish Pavilion for the 1939 New York World's Fair. For a brief moment the public caught a glimpse of the emerging Scandinavian style that would develop and proliferate in the decades following World War II.

Right and below: Modernism meets Nature in chair No. 406. For Alvar Aalto, the use of wood in both design and architecture was an expression of Finnish national identity. In the wider context of European Modernism, it was also a way of humanizing the sometimes harsh, intransigent effects of a functionalist aesthetic.

LANDI

1939
Hans Coray

The Landi chair got its name after becoming one of the most remarked-upon objects shown at the Schweizerische Landesausstellung (Swiss National Exhibition) in Zurich in 1939. Its designer was the now little-known Hans Coray (1906–91), who was part of the Swiss group of avant-garde designers and artists known as the Zürcher Schule der Konkreten (Zurich School of Concrete Artists).

The Landi was designed as an advertisement for Switzerland's burgeoning aluminium industry and exploited both the physical and aesthetic qualities of that medium to the full. The flexible yet strong shell is made from a single mass-produced shape, while the legs are utterly rigid. The circular apertures cut into the backrest give the chair an airy quality as well as giving structural strength to the form. The chair has an attractive crystalline sheen – the result of what were then cutting-edge heat and chemical treatments.

Lightweight, weatherproof and beautifully proportioned, the Landi has spawned hundreds of imitations and remains an icon of Swiss industrial design. Yet despite the success of his chair, Coray largely abandoned design in the 1950s.

Right: The aluminium Landi was lightweight, robust and easy to clean. The L-shaped seat cradled on a four-legged base would have an enduring impact on subsequent stackable chair designs.

LCW – LOUNGE CHAIR WOOD

1945
Charles and Ray Eames

Soon after their arrival in the forward-thinking and optimistic Los Angeles of the early 1940s, husband and wife Charles (1907–78) and Ray (1912–88) Eames began experimenting with plywood structures. Using wood and glue smuggled out of the MGM Studio workshops, where Charles worked as a film-set designer, they laminated away in the seclusion of their apartment. By 1945 they had created a coded range of furniture that included the DCW (Dining Chair Wood) and LCW (Lounge Chair Wood).

The couple's initial intention had been to fashion the seat and backrest out of a single angled sheet. However, the plywood proved prone to cracking when bent at such a sharp angle, and their solution was to split the form into a separate seat and backrest joined by an elegant twisting plywood spine. Rubber fixings at the joints allowed for a slight flexing that could respond to the body shape of the sitter – a pioneering feature that demonstrated the Eames' determination to design furniture that was as good to use as it was good to look at and cheap to buy.

Robust, comfortable and refreshingly affordable, the LCW was the perfect chair for the United States's growing population of homemaking young families in the post-World War II era. For the Eames, it proved the major breakthrough in their career.

Right: Constructed from several components of laminated wood, the Eames's LCW provided modern and affordable style for the United States's booming market of young, style-conscious homemakers.

LAR, DAR AND RAR

Another of Charles and Ray Eames's aspirations (see pages 40–1) was to design furniture that could adapt to the owner's changing needs. The 'mix and match' LAR (Lounge Armchair Rod), DAR (Dining Armchair Rod) and RAR (Rocker Armchair Rod), developed for the Low-Cost Furniture Design Competition held at New York's Museum of Modern Art in 1948, were brilliant demonstrations of how this might be achieved.

The fibreglass-reinforced plastic seats could be attached to any of three components – an elegant 'Eiffel Tower'-shaped base; tapering metal rod legs; or two curved bands of wood, or rockers (see picture on page 2). An innovative welded shock mount developed by the US automotive giant Chrysler was used to attach the two basic components, allowing for some movement between seat and legs. Initially the chairs were available only in a somewhat dispiriting grey, grey-green and beige, but this range was quickly amplified.

Manufactured by Herman Miller in collaboration with Zenith Plastics, LAR, DAR and RAR were the first mass-produced plastic chairs. The Eames's playful, inventive designs were harbingers of the new 'Contemporary' style in interior design, with its emphasis on lightness, fluidity and open-plan living.

Right: The fibreglass seat of this cheap-to-produce yet stylish chair could be mixed and matched with different bases – here on the so-called 'Eiffel Tower' base. Below: The same seat mounted on a four-legged base.

ANTELOPE

In 1951, with the air-raid sirens long silenced but rationing still largely in place, the Festival of Britain turned London into a hotbed of new ideas and starry-eyed optimism. The Festival's principal aims – in the centenary year of the Great Exhibition – was to promote British design and industry and to provide, as one government minister, Herbert Morrison, declared, 'a tonic for the nation' with its promise of a brighter future.

Almost 8.5 million people visited the remodelled South Bank and its array of glass-walled pavilions and airy public buildings, including the still-extant Royal Festival Hall. It was a multisensual and immersive experience from the moment you entered the Festival grounds, and this included where you walked, what you saw, even where you sat down. The carefully considered seating included the now-iconic Antelope chair by Ernest Race (1913–64).

With its whimsical frame of bent-steel rods, its seat of moulded plywood, painted in the Festival colours of yellow, blue, red or grey, and its balled feet inspired by molecular physics, the Antelope was a jaunty addition to the grey concrete terraces that surrounded the Festival Hall. It had a companion piece, in the form of the stackable Springbok chair. Both pieces went into commercial production after the end of the Festival.

Right: The playful arabesques of the Antelope chair capture the optimistic spirit of early-1950s Britain. Below: Ernest Race produced a bench version of the chair, also used as seating in the South Bank's Festival of Britain grounds.

DKR WIRE MESH CHAIR

1951
Charles and Ray Eames

By the early 1950s Charles and Ray Eames (see pages 40–3) were turning their innovative design skills to structures made from bent and welded steel. Like the plywood chairs of the previous decade, the DKR used technologies developed for military use during World War II. The concave shape of the DKR echoes that of the Eames's plastic seating but is here constructed as a series of horizontal and vertical shiny steel contour lines. The structure is cleverly braced within a thicker steel rim that visually hems in the mesh structure and gives it strength. Although heavy to lift, the result is an airy piece of furniture that looks like a 3D drawing.

Once again the Eames applied their clever mix-and-match system of alternative bases so the DKR could perform different functions for different people in different places. On steel stackable legs the chair was a storable and movable addition to a meeting room. On the elegant 'Eiffel Tower' base it could add modern grace to any domestic dining room. And, for the icing on the cake, the chair could be provided with a wide variety of covers designed by Alexander Girard (1907–93) – from glamorous black leather to a range of patterned fabrics.

The Wire Mesh chair was manufactured by Herman Miller until 1967 and reissued in 2001. Research into wire seating was continued by Harry Bertoia in his Diamond chair (see pages 48–9).

Right: Charles and Ray Eames's Wire Mesh chair on an 'Eiffel Tower' base. Such light and airy designs came to typify the 1950s 'Contemporary' style.

DIAMOND

'If you look at these chairs, you will see that they are mainly made of air, just like light sculptures,' said Harry Bertoia of what is perhaps his best-known creation, the Diamond chair. 'Space goes clean through them.'

During the 1940s, Bertoia (1915–78), an Italian-born designer, had worked alongside Charles and Ray Eames in the development of moulded plywood and played a key role in the creation of the LCW (see pages 40–1). In 1950, however, he set up his own studio in Pennsylvania and soon after developed a collection for the pioneering US design company Kroll in which the Diamond chair was the signature piece.

Despite a patent dispute with Herman Miller – the manufacturer of the Eames's own wire chair – the Diamond chair proved a huge commercial success and subsequently enabled Bertoia to devote himself exclusively to sculpture.

Right: The diagrammatic wire-mesh structure of the Diamond chair enables it to perform its function with a minimum of volume and material.

ROCKING STOOL

The Rocking stool that literally rocked! Here was another chair that, like Harry Bertoia's Diamond chair (see pages 48–9), crossed the boundaries between design and sculpture – unsurprisingly, perhaps, as its creator was the Japanese-American sculptor Isamu Noguchi (1904–88).

Throughout his career Noguchi combined a sculptural way of thinking with the formal side of design, this synthesis resulting in an extraordinary range of projects that included landscape architecture, stage sets for the dancer Martha Graham, and mass-manufactured lighting and furniture for Herman Miller and Kroll. The goblet form of the Kroll-produced Rocking stool echoes that of an African *djembe* drum, while the connecting steel rods paid tribute to Bertoia's wirework. Cambered bases allow the stools to rock gently in all directions – an ingenious playful touch in tune with the spirit of the age.

The Rocking stool was designed at a time when social structures, music and fashion were all bending to the forces of cultural change. From Elvis to Eames, the world was accepting different ways of listening, living and behaving. Why sit up straight when you could be swaying to a new and youthful rhythm?

Right: A contemporary photograph demonstrating the kinetic possibilities of the Rocking stool. Below: Isamu Noguchi's design blurred the boundaries between product and sculpture.

MODEL 3107

1955
Arne Jacobsen

It may now be tamed as a somewhat hackneyed choice for many a retro-Modernist canteen or café, but the Model 3107 (part of the Series 7 group) started its life as something altogether more interesting and principled.

Created by the Danish architect Arne Jacobsen (1902–71) in 1955, the Model 3107 chair followed the *Gesamtkunstwerk* ideology that the design of exterior and interior spaces should be seamlessly conceived. The 3107, together with its Series 7 siblings, was essentially an evolution of Jacobsen's three-legged Ant of 1952, an Eames-inspired moulded-plywood chair designed for the Danish pharmaceutical company Novo Nordisk. The new chair, however, proved even more successful and became the standard-bearer of the so-called 'Danish Modern' style.

Jacobsen's creation won a kind of vicarious notoriety when, in 1963, Lewis Morley photographed Christine Keeler, one of the chief protagonists of the Profumo Affair, sitting astride what looks very much like a 3107 chair, its hourglass back both concealing and echoing the model's naked body. Recent researches at the Victoria and Albert Museum have shown that the 'Keeler chair' now in its possession was in fact one of the many 'knockoff' replicas of the Model 3107 produced at around this time.

Right: The Series 7 Model 3107 in a contemporary Modernist-derived setting. Arne Jacobsen's spare yet sensual design works perfectly in this marriage between interior and exterior spaces.

TULIP

With the chill of the Cold War in the air, a bright white future was becoming the present. A meteorite's throw from the sci-fi style of the 1960s, the Finnish-American Eero Saarinen (1910–61) created the Tulip chair on which André Courrèges's spacewear-clad fashion models would later sit.

The Tulip chair is a single statement in white plastic that seems to grow, flower-like, out of the floor to bloom into a body-embracing cup. Despite its organic imagery, however, there is nothing hand-crafted about this design. The chair has come into existence scientifically, through chemicals cast in moulds and morphed, to be born into an anxious new world that was deeply ambivalent about new technologies.

The son of the eminent Finnish architect Eliel Saarinen, Eero was an accomplished architect and designer in his own right. His architectural projects included the TWA Flight Center (now the JetBlue Flight Center) at New York's John F Kennedy Airport, which, like many of his works, featured futuristic-looking curves. He was a friend of both Charles and Ray Eames and Harry Bertoia, and he shared their zest for creating fluid organic forms using the most concise manufacturing methods possible.

The Tulip chair won celebrity in popular culture when it was used in the TV sci-fi series *Star Trek* (1966–9).

Right: A chair for the Space Age. In Saarinen's Tulip chair, organic form springs from artificial origins. Below: The futuristic chair also came in a version with a narrow back, suitable for the dining room and a spaceship flight deck.

EAMES LOUNGE CHAIR –
THE 670

1956
Charles and Ray Eames

Charles and Ray Eames devoted much of their creative lives to developing objects and furniture that could be mass-produced and sold at affordable prices. An exception, however, was the luxurious 1956 Eames 670 inspired by the traditional English club chair and produced with a matching ottoman. Despite such sybaritic connotations, however, Charles wrote that his intention was to create a chair with the 'warm, receptive look of a well-used first baseman's mitt'.

The 670 lounge chair essentially consists of three shells – the headrest, the backrest and the seat – each made from five fused layers of plywood plus two layers of Brazilian rosewood veneer. The armrests made the same innovative use of shock mounts that the couple had employed in designs of a decade earlier (see pages 42–3). Unusually, too, the upholstery was attached to the chair seat by a zipper.

As with other Eames designs, the 670 quickly generated a host of low-quality imitations. Nevertheless, the chair has had an enormous impact on the development of furniture design right across the spectrum – from bachelor pad to boardroom, a new look was launched that combined utility, modernity and black-leather comfort.

Right: Like a 'well-used first baseman's mitt'. Ray Eames's description of his and his wife's design hardly does justice to the style and luxury of the 670.

MEZZADRO

1954–7
Achille and Pier
Giacomo Castiglioni

In the late 1950s Achille Castiglioni (1918–2002) and his brother Pier Giacomo (1913–68) threw down a challenge to the Italian design industry. For Castiglioni, 'design demands observation', and it was the everyday objects around them, together with the ways in which people interacted with those objects, that most deeply inspired the Castiglionis' designs.

One of the brothers' most iconic pieces is the Mezzadro chair, which was a kind of design equivalent of the Duchamp's 'ready-mades'. Composed out of the seat and crossbar from a vintage Italian tractor, the Mezzadro, however, is not just a witty, surrealistic exercise in appropriation and redesign but also a thoughtful essay about how people really behave and how design might respond more fluidly to such behaviours. Thus of a contemporaneous stool made out of a bicycle seat – the Sella – Achille remarked, 'When I use a payphone, I like to move around, but I would also like to sit – but not completely.'

Considered too radical by manufacturers at the time, the Mezzadro was not put into production until 1983 when Zanotta was finally persuaded to issue the original design.

Right: With a seat taken from a tractor placed on a bent-metal cantilevered stand, the Mezzadro chair comments on cultural evolution and the relationship between people and changing technology.

SUPERLEGGERA

In the late 1920s the Italian polymath designer Giò Ponti (1891–1979) wrote, 'Industry is the style of the twentieth century, its mode of creation' – wise words that were to prove increasingly resonant as the century progressed, as Italy and the rest of the world surrendered heart and soul to technology. For all that, one of the primary concerns behind all of Ponti's own work – be it architecture, furniture or lighting – was the promotion of joy and quality of life – together with a poetic predilection for the light and airy.

Industrialism, lightness and *la dolce vita* were combined in the Superleggera ('superlight') chair of 1957, on which Ponti laboured for well nigh a decade. Its traditional shape was inspired by the Chiavari chairs scattered along the beaches of the Italian Riviera, and it could be made in large numbers both cheaply and easily. Its most noteworthy quality, of course, was its extraordinary lightness, in terms of both its weight and its aesthetic appeal – the result of its slender ashwood frame and pale cane seating.

The Superleggera is still produced by its original manufacturer, the Italian high-end design company Cassina.

Right: The traditional form and exquisite use of modern materials in the Superleggera chair evoke the Italian delight in *la dolce vita*.

POLYPROP

Since the early 1960s the Polyprop must have infiltrated just about every UK school, hospital, factory and village hall. This has been *the* seat of learning, resting, lunching and waiting – so ubiquitous, indeed, that it quickly became near-invisible. While we may now take the Polyprop for granted, in reality, of course, it was a technical tour de force.

The Polyprop's creator was Robin Day (1915–) – with his wife, the textile designer Lucienne Day (1917–), part of a design duo that was widely seen as the British counterpart to the US husband-and-wife team Charles and Ray Eames. With the Polyprop, Day set out to make a cheaper version of the Eames' fibreglass chairs (see pages 42–3) and, to do so, he exploited injection moulding – a mass-production process that had boomed after World War II but which up to that point had not been widely used for furniture.

The chair's shell was formed out of a single piece of polypropylene – hence, of course, the name – and was based on a tubular-steel base, with splayed legs – a feature it shared with many other 'Contemporary'-styled chairs of the time, Ernest Race's Antelope for instance (see pages 44–5). It was easy to move and carry, stack and clean, and could be manufactured both quickly and in high numbers. To date it is estimated that some 14 million Polyprops have been made.

Right and below: The familiar injection-moulded form of the Polyprop is testament to the design skills and technical-problem solving of Robin Day.

UNIVERSALE

During the early 1960s the Italian industrial designer and former artist Joe Colombo (1931–71) became obsessed with the problem of how to make a single-form mass-production chair. Initially he experimented with aluminium but he eventually succeeded with the strong and resilient plastic known as ABS (which from 1963, incidentally, was also used to make the children's toy Lego). The Universale was born.

Colombo liked to describe himself as a 'creator of the environment of the future' and the Universale certainly had a futuristic, Space Age feel. Its bright vibrant colours and playful rounded forms, too, gave it an affinity with the Pop art of the period. Another of Colombo's abiding concerns was variability, and the Universale's system of interchangeable screw-on legs could be used to alter the height of the chair and thus change its function – from tall bar stool to dining-room chair.

As the decade progressed, Colombo would experiment with modular furniture design to create dynamic, fluid living spaces.

Right: The Universale was the result of designer Joe Colombo's efforts to make a chair that could be cast as one piece. Its extra attraction was a system of detachable screw-on legs that could transform the seat from a standard-height chair to a high stool.

BLOW CHAIR

1967
DDL

A chair that could go bang in a world that had gone pop …

In the 1960s plastics, technology and mass manufacturing were transforming how people dressed, travelled, communicated and lived. The mass availability of cheap consumer goods changed people's attitudes towards the everyday objects around them, and a throwaway mentality rapidly took hold. People were living for the moment – after all, wasn't the world about to be blasted to oblivion anyway?

The Blow chair epitomized the 1960s trend for mass-manufactured disposable living and challenged conventional notions of craft, permanence and cost. It was designed by DDL, a Milan-based studio established by Donato D'Urbino (1935–), Jonathan De Pas (1932–91) and Paolo Lomazzi (1936–), and was manufactured by Zanotta. Used indoors or out, this inflatable PVC chair was fun, affordable … and dispensable. It was never intended to be permanent, and even came with a puncture-repair kit to deal with the inevitable blowout.

All the same, its colourful Michelin Man-inspired aesthetic and frivolous sense of fun has given it longlife commercial appeal that has more than justified the design being reissued and much copied up to the present day.

Right: DDL's cheap and cheerful inflatable Blow chair brought fun into furnishing. Below: In this cartoon even its own designers found the funny side.

VERY EASY TO BE MANUFACTURED !

SACCO

1968
Piero Gatti,
Cesare Paolini &
Franco Teodoro

In the late 1960s Italy increasingly positioned itself at the forefront of contemporary design, as companies such as Cassina and Zanotta showed themselves prepared to take up what appeared to be groundbreaking, quirky or even downright impractical designs. Zanotta took just such a risk with the Sacco and found itself with a hit on its hands.

On one level the Sacco was an exercise in iconoclasm – a piece of design that was anti-design, whose most crucial quality was its form*less*ness. But on another it was fun and practical, an object that both responded to, and facilitated, the laidback, youthful lifestyles of the 1960s.

Designed by Piero Gatti (1940–), Cesare Paolini (1937–) and Franco Teodoro (1939–), the Sacco consisted of a black leather or fabric bag (*sacco* in Italian) filled with hundreds of tiny polystyrene spheres. It did away with almost every aspect of the traditional chair – seat, back, armrests, legs – but instead moulded itself to the shape of the user's body whatever posture he or she chose. Infinitely malleable, easily portable, it could become a chair, a chaise longue, a footstool, or even a kind of domestic sculpture. The progenitor of countless 'bean bags', the Sacco inaugurated a whole new genre of furniture.

Right: The mother of all bean bags, the Sacco – designed by the Italian design trio Piero Gatti, Cesare Paolini and Franco Teodoro and manufactured by Zanotta. Unlike its more downmarket offspring, the original Sacco was often made from luxurious leather.

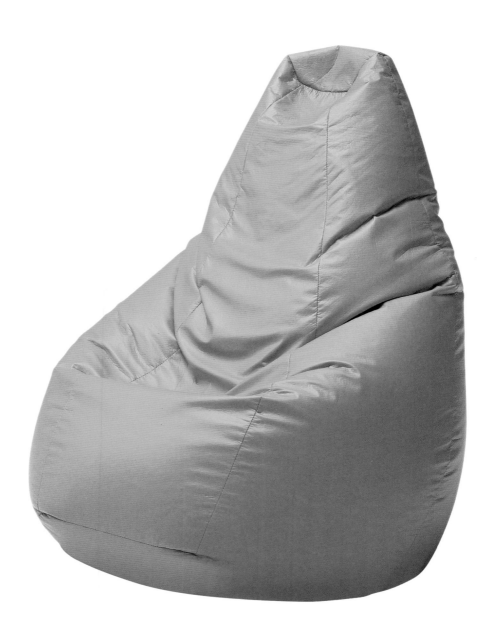

PANTON

Sleek and sexy, this tongue-like sliver of a chair made its first appearance in the Danish design journal *Mobilia* in 1967, though it had been in development for many years previously. It caused an immediate sensation, striking just the right note of playful, sensuous optimism, and was technically pioneering, too, being the first cantilevered seat to be made out of just one piece of plastic.

Its designer was the architect Verner Panton (1926–98), who at the beginning of the 1950s had briefly worked in the studio of Arne Jacobsen (see pages 52–3). In 1956 Panton produced a plywood cantilevered stackable chair – the S-chair – and two years later he made sketches for what was essentially a plastic evolution of the S and an early version of the Panton. It was not until the middle of the next decade, however, that the chair underwent intensive development, with the support of Willi Fehlbaum, the founder of the German (and later Swiss) manufacturing company Vitra. The chair was initially formed of fibreglass-reinforced polyester resin, but since the 1980s it has been made of polyurethane rigid foam.

The Panton chair, like Jacobsen's Model 3107 before it, went on to find a certain notoriety when, in 1970, it was used as a prop in the British fashion magazine *Nova* in a photo-essay entitled 'How to undress in front of your husband'.

Right: With its streamlined profile that echoes the curved outline of a seated human body, the Panton chair is sensual, stylish and fun.

UP5 DONNA

1969
Gaetano Pesce

Break the seal and watch it grow. Compressed to a tenth of its full size for easy transit, the Up5 expanded to its full dimensions in front of your eyes as soon as the vacuum packaging was opened. The avant-garde Italian architect Gaetano Pesce (1939–), who designed the chair for B&B Italia as part of the seven-model Up series, described this rethinking of manufacture and assemblage as 'transformation furniture'.

The Up5 was the perfect riposte to the rigid plastic chairs that had proliferated up to that time. Unabashedly, voluptuously feminine, the Donna ('lady') came with an attached ball-shaped ottoman – the Up6 – that was rather kitschly supposed to symbolize society's subjection of women. The combination of moulded polyurethane foam and stretch fabric gave it the texture and comfort of upholstered furniture while retaining a sense of the poppy modernity of the time.

The chair had a sudden and unexpected resurgence of popularity when, after its reissue in 2000, it starred as the diary-room seat in the 2002 series of the UK reality-TV show *Big Brother*.

Right: The curvaceous forms of the Up5 – the Donna, or Lady – enfold the sitter in a womblike embrace. Below: The Up5 with its spherical footstool or ottoman.

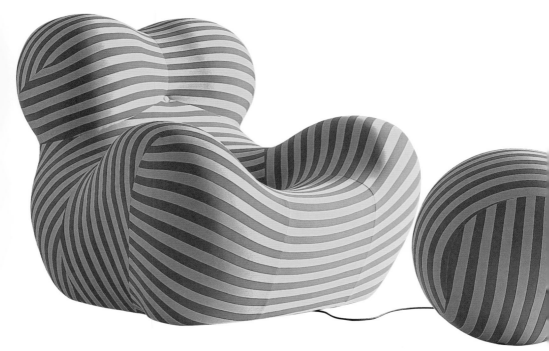

BIRILLO

In 1969, as ghostly images of the NASA astronaut Neil Armstrong were beamed back to earth, the Space Age seemed to have become a reality – it was no longer just a theory or a fashion trend. Technology was working, and it was transforming every aspect of human life. In Italy the work of Joe Colombo (1931–70), as he continued his mission 'to invent the future' (see pages 64–5), seemed best to encapsulate the fevered optimism of the times.

The modestly named Birillo (simply the Italian for 'bar stool') is one of Colombo's most visually seductive designs. This high-seated chair – made from stainless steel, fibreglass and leather – was primarily intended to grace the interiors of fashionable early 1970s bars and offices. It offered comfort and support with an almost robotic simplicity, while its sculpted X-marks-the-spot base featured concealed casters that enabled it to glide as smoothly through space as any sci-fi rocket ship.

The chair was designed during the development of Colombo's ambitious Visiona project in which he sought to create a 'living cell' – a flexible, dynamic self-contained habitat. Sadly, the designer's sudden death from heart failure in 1971 brought a premature end to his visionary and inspirational experiments.

Right: With its cool geometric aesthetic, Joe Colombo's Birillo stool evokes Space Age modernity. Would it be too much to muse that the moon is referenced in the white disc-like backrest?

SYNTHESIS 45

1971
Ettore Sottsass

By the 1950s the traditional office, with its stuffy constricted rooms and heavy wooden desks and chairs, had become distinctly outmoded. What was needed was something altogether more in keeping with the times, something that would both promote a more dynamic business environment and appeal to hip and youthful office workers. In 1958 the leading Italian manufacturer Olivetti hired the flamboyant designer Ettore Sottsass (1917–2007) as its chief design consultant, and charged him with the task of revamping its range of electronic equipment and office furnishings for the Pop Age.

The fruits of the Olivetti-Sottsass collaboration proved both technically innovative and visually seductive – the lightweight, lipstick-red Valentine typewriter of 1970 being a case in point, though Sottsass himself would later dismiss it as 'too obvious, like a girl wearing a very short skirt'. With its paintbox-bright colours and chunky silhouette, the jaunty Synthesis 45 swivel office chair was no doubt obvious, too, but after the dank, cramped offices of yesteryear it was a breath of fresh air.

Right: With its strong colours and robust form, the Synthesis 45 was the perfect addition to a forward-looking office of the early 1970s.

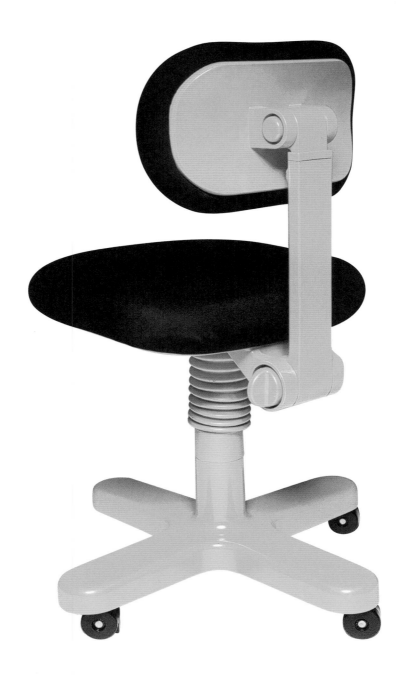

OMKSTAK

The British furniture designer Rodney Kinsman (1943–) may not be a household name but his OMKSTAK chair was one of the most popular chairs of the 1970s. A founding member of the London design studio OMK, Kinsman first made his name in the mid-1960s with his stylish F Range chair. Throughout his career his furniture has been marked by its uncompromising rationalism, though his creations are never without a certain tough-minded poetry.

The OMKSTAK stacking chair was Kinsman's first design for the mass-production contract market and was a brilliant exercise in rational form. Featuring a pierced pressed-steel seat and back on a continuous tubular frame, it was light, durable and fireproof and could be stacked 25-plus high. In form the OMKSTAK may have owed a certain debt to Hans Coray's Landi chair of 1939 (see pages 38–9), but the paintbox colours of its epoxy-coated seats added more than a splash of Pop art contemporaneity.

The OMKSTAK remained in production for several decades and in 2008 it returned to the British high street courtesy of Habitat.

Right: The brightly coloured pierced-metal seat and backrest of the OMKSTAK chair manages to suggest both fun and practicality.

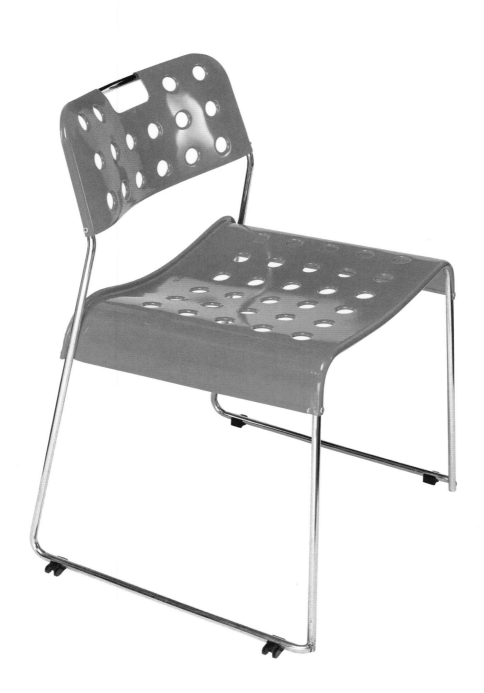

WIGGLE SIDE CHAIR

1972
Frank O Gehry

'I began to play with it, to glue it together and to cut it into shapes with a handsaw and a pocket knife ...' Thus Frank Gehry (1929–) described his experiments with corrugated-cardboard furniture in the 1960s that eventually resulted in the Wiggle side chair. Gehry, of course, is best known as an architect – for spectacular buildings such as the Guggenheim Museum in Bilbao and the Dancing House in Prague. However, throughout his career he has also experimented with designs for furniture.

Gehry's first line of furniture – named Easy Edges – was produced between 1969 and 1973 and gave a whole new aesthetic to an everyday, utilitarian material. The undoubted masterpiece of the series was the Wiggle side chair. Composed of some 60 layers of cardboard glued and screwed together, its fluid curves resemble a low-tech reinterpretation of the laminated wood techniques associated with designers such as Charles and Ray Eames (see pages 40–3) and Arne Jacobsen (see pages 52–3) a couple of decades or so earlier.

However, its meticulous craftsmanship and subtle engineering save the Wiggle from being a mere exercise in whimsy. A couple of generations before ecological design once more came to the fore, Gehry demonstrated the strength and versatility of an underused and potentially 'green' material.

Right: The Wiggle side chair – Frank Gehry's furniture is every bit as innovative, playful and surprising as his architecture.

SUPPORTO CHAIR

1979
Fred Scott

As its italianized name suggests, the Supporto chair was made to meet ergonomic needs. Designed by Fred Scott (1942–2001) for Hille International, Britain's leading manufacturer of contemporary furniture, it represented a drive to compete with the office furniture designed by Charles and Ray Eames (see pages 40–3) for the US-based company Herman Miller. Here was a British design thoroughly informed by scientific and consumer research and consumer testing, and carefully marketed to an audience that was becoming increasingly concerned with the practicalities of improving working conditions and healthier living.

With its casters positioned at the tips of a broad, five-pronged base, the chair can be propelled from a seated position without toppling. The long and rigid armrests cradle the sitter and provide sturdy handles to clasp when standing up. The leather-clad cushioned seat and backrest provide comfort even for long periods of sitting, while the curvature of the backrest supports the back and encourages good posture.

The Supporto became an almost instant classic and marked Scott out as one of the leading British designers of his generation. His career, however, was to be blighted by serious illness, preventing him from fulfilling the potential that the Supporto had so richly promised.

Right: With its clean lines and uninterrupted planes, the Supporto chair has a utilitarian chic that conveys both practicality and elegance. Below: The curved back of the Supporto suggests the ergonomic sophistication that went into this British office chair.

ROVER

In a London still braced by the anarchic energy of Punk but as yet unaltered by the winds of 1980s regeneration, a self-reliant individualism was forming as people mended and made do their way through the vicissitudes of inner-city living. It was a mood that was perfectly captured by the Rover chair, which was essentially a collage of two existing products – a Rover 200 seat, squirrelled out of a junkyard, and a 1930s-style Kee Klamp tubular-pipe frame. A fusion, in short, of two ready-mades.

The Rover chair was the first piece of furniture produced by the Israeli-born architect Ron Arad (1951–), who had only recently emerged from years of study at the Architecture Association in London. Rather than paying his dues in an architectural practice, Arad preferred to set up his own design business, whose very name – One Off – suggested his outright refusal to compromise.

As a furniture-maker, Arad was self-taught, part of a generation of hands-on designer-makers who resorted to raw and rugged materials and techniques out of economic necessity. As a consequence, the Rover chair may lack the slickness of the earlier ready-made designs of Achille Castiglioni (see pages 58–9), but it more than makes up for that in sheer energy and verve.

Right: The Rover chair helped establish Ron Arad as part of a new wave of maverick designers in the early 1980s. Below: A design sketch showing the car seat nestled within the tubular-metal base.

QUEEN ANNE CHAIR

1985
Robert Venturi

Like Frank Gehry (see pages 80–1), Robert Venturi (1925–) is much better known as an architect but has also produced furniture that is expressive of his ideas and idiosyncrasies. Like other architects and designers of the 1980s, Venturi rebelled against the dictates of Modernism to develop styles that were playful, decorative, ostentatious and historicist. To Ludwig Mies van der Rohe's famous maxim 'Less is more', he retorted 'Less is a bore'. For Venturi, 'complexity' and 'contradiction' are far better watchwords than functionalism and rationalism in the postmodern age.

In his first range of furniture, issued from the late 1970s to the early 1980s, Venturi raided a whole pattern book of major historical styles – from Sheraton and Chippendale to Gothic Revival and Art Nouveau. In the Queen Anne chair he turned to the feminized elegance of the early eighteenth century to create a chair that looks forward just as much as it dares to look back. With its boldly drawn outline and squat, boxlike form, the chair echoes the powerful silhouettes of much of Venturi's architecture – the classicizing bravura of works such as the National Gallery's Sainsbury Wing in London. To this Venturi adds a riot of colour and outrageous pattern that is sometimes confined to the upholstery, but sometimes invades the frame as well.

The Queen Anne chair is far from being a pastiche, however: it is an example of how designers can draw inspiration from anywhere and any time and still make work that is forward-looking and meaningful.

Right: Appropriation and fusion of historic and modern influences are evident in the boxlike and flat-faceted Queen Anne chair.
Below: When seen in profile, Robert Venturi's chair has a surprisingly slender silhouette that contrasts with the broad expanse of the design when seen from the front.

HOW HIGH THE MOON

1986
Shiro Kuramata

Combining the solidity of metal with the transparency of air, a generosity of volume with the weightlessness of light, Shiro Kuramata's How High the Moon chair is a series of visual and structural contradictions.

The chair is constructed out of a perforated nickel-plated steel mesh that would typically be exploited for its strength but kept hidden out of sight. Here, however, the Japan-based designer Shiro Kuramata (1934–91) imbues the utilitarian with a poetic, dreamlike delicacy to create a shimmering representation of volume that you can see both into and beyond. The result is a chair that seems almost to dematerialize before our eyes – as evanescent, indeed, as silvery moonlight.

In its combination of technical innovation with a spare yet lyrical aesthetic, the How High the Moon embodies the spirit of much 1980s Japanese design – one that helped alert the West to alternative traditions and discourses to those of mainstream European and American Modernism.

Right: The precision-made metal-mesh skin of the How High the Moon chair makes for a shimmering and poetic representation of volume and form.

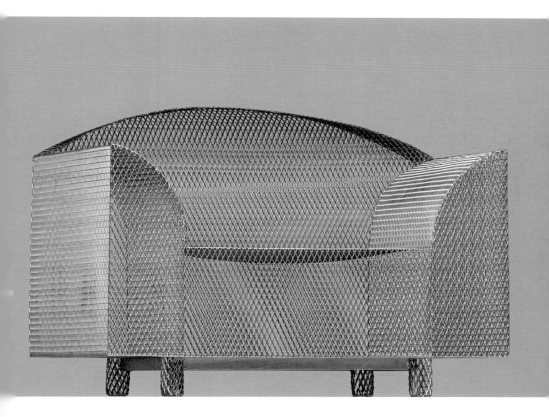

PLYWOOD CHAIR

1988
Jasper Morrison

Early on in his career, the British designer Jasper Morrison (1959–) had to make and build his own designs, but nevertheless insisted on using industrial processes to do so, rather than resorting to the hand-craft methods otherwise usually favoured by impecunious designers. This involved making the most of whatever materials, equipment and processes were available and turning his limitations into strengths.

Morrison undertook the design for the Plywood chair as part of an installation in Berlin called 'Some New Items for the Home'. All that he had to hand was an electric jigsaw, a set of ship's curves and a bountiful supply of plywood. The project consisted of cutting out shapes in plywood and then reassembling them to make a sturdy, functional three-dimensional structure. Simple as this might sound, the Plywood chair nonetheless required, and shows, an acute and sensitive understanding of form, and manages to evoke the essence of a traditional chair with the minimum of fuss and embellishment. The colour and texture of the birch veneer are as subdued and unassuming as its form.

The Plywood chair was later put into production by the Swiss furniture company Vitra.

Right: The sedate and sensitive form of the Plywood chair evokes the spirit of a traditional chair with minimal expression and fuss. Below: A design sketch showing two Plywood chairs and a table.

S-CHAIR

1991
Tom Dixon

Self-taught and self-motivated, Tom Dixon (1959–) emerged in the 1980s as one of the UK's new wave of hands-on, make-it-yourself designers. Approaching the creative process with an explorative try-it-and-see mentality, he worked on more than 50 prototypes – experimenting with materials as diverse as wicker, discarded tyre rubber, paper and copper – before finally coming up with the now-celebrated S-chair.

The S, of course, owes much to the cantilevered technology explored more than three decades earlier, in classics such as the B32 and the Panton chair. At the same time, however, it discarded their sleek Pop sensibility for something altogether more raw and imprecise, trading industrialized refinement for handcrafted, organic chic. The chair's lacquered-metal frame is covered in a woven marsh straw or wicker, whose uneven texture defies Modernist conventions of perfection and geometry.

Initially, the S-chairs were made solely by Dixon himself but they were eventually put into production by the high-end Italian manufacturer Cappellini.

Right: Tom Dixon's S-chair owes an undoubted debt to the Panton chair, but eschews sensual perfection for textural and visual imprecision. Below: Front on, the chair has a sculptural quality evocative of traditional African crafts.

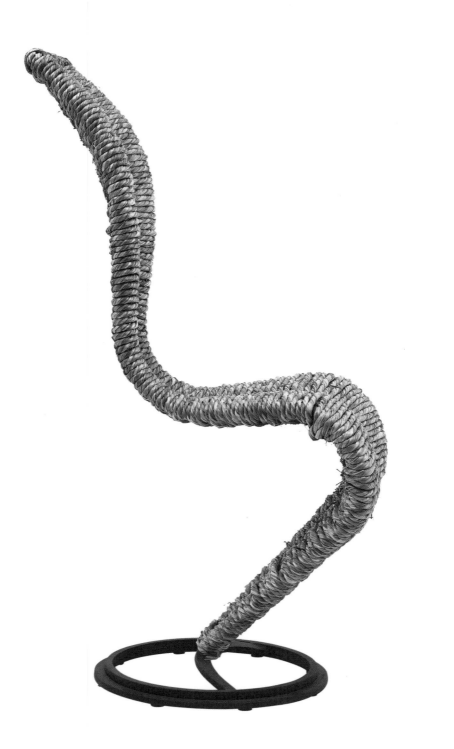

LOUIS 20

1991
Philippe Starck

Philippe Starck (1949–) is the celebrated French designer of knowing design icons, of playful postmodernist pranks and New Design *jeu d'esprit*. To some tastes, Starck's mass-produced lines – quintessentially, the spider-like Juicy Salif lemon squeezer (1990) made by Alessi – may be infuriatingly mannered and, practically speaking, redundant, but from time to time his jokes can take on an iconoclastic grandeur and even an unexpected emotion.

Fusing a polypropylene seat and front legs with tubular aluminium back legs, the Louis 20 blasphemously hybridizes the two key strands in the development of the twentieth-century chair and throws down a challenge to the purism – and, Starck would add, puritanism – that lies at the heart of Modernism. Not content with that, the chair also gently satirizes the enduring French love of *le style Louis Quinze* with all its Rococo trappings.

For all that, the Louis 20 looks good. It possesses the technical rigour synonymous with Starck's work and has a sleek, urbane beauty that transcends its 'designer' credentials. The fact that the plastic seat and legs have an anthropomorphic quality adds a final joyful chuckle to any appreciation of the chair.

Right and below: *Jeu d'esprit* – Philippe Starck's Louis 20 is a daring yet successful fusion of the two stars of Modernist chair design – tubular metal and plastic.

AERON OFFICE CHAIR

1992
Donald T Chadwick
and William Stumpf

As people began to spend more and more time at their desks in the new computer-age office, the provision of a new ergonomic chair became crucial, not only in terms of comfort but for long-term health reasons as well. To meet these criteria the US manufacturer Herman Miller turned to two long-established designers, Donald T Chadwick (1936–) and William Stumpf (1936–2006), with whom it had already collaborated on the Equa office chair in 1984.

There followed several years of research and development, involving teams of ergonomists, orthopaedic specialists and physical therapists, together with a detailed anthropometric survey of 224 people. The designers set out to create a chair that would be a 'metaphor for the human form in the visual as well as the tactile sense'. The result was the Aeron office chair, whose curvaceous biomorphic structure follows and adapts to the contours of the human body. More surprisingly, perhaps, the Aeron is neither padded nor upholstered – relying on its form alone to offer support and comfort.

The organic forms of the Aeron owe something, of course, to the heritage of Charles and Ray Eames (see pages 40–3), but the airy looks implied in its name were in keeping with a much more contemporary concern in architecture and technology with the aesthetics and values of transparency. In this the Aeron predated Jonathan Ive's translucent Bondi-blue Apple iMac (1998) by several years.

Right: The Aeron office chair was designed as a desirable, high-tech remedy for the ailments attendant on modern working life.

FPE CHAIR

1997
Ron Arad

Poppy and bright but technically innovative, too, Ron Arad's (1951–) 1997 chair for the Italian manufacturer Kartell is Fantastic, Plastic, Elastic …

It's *fantastic* because of the technical prowess that allows the single sheet of twisting plastic to be cleanly fused between two parallel curvaceous aluminium tubes. It's *plastic* because a continuous brightly coloured strip of plastic gives the chair a joyful presence that chimed in well with the optimism and retro tastes of the late 1990s. It's *elastic* because the chair morphs around the body when weight is put on it, but springs back into a standardized shape afterwards, allowing it to be neatly stacked up to eight units high.

Acronyms aside, the FPE signalled Arad's increasing concern with the biomorphic in his work, as he continued to erase the borders between sculpture, art and design.

Right: Fantastic Plastic Elastic spells out the acronym that describes these flexible, groovy-looking chairs.

AIR-CHAIR

Today Jasper Morrison's (1959–) pastel-hued Air-chair graces many a smart modern café and public space. With its moulded polypropylene aesthetic and gently pastiched shape, it can seem clonelike when seen in groups, but nonetheless has a quirky personality all of its own …

The Air-chair is evidence of Morrison's ongoing love affair with industrial techniques (see pages 90–1), utilizing a gas-injected polypropylene casting technique first introduced to him by Alberto Perazza, the owner of Italian manufacturer Magis. The result of Morrison's endeavours is a sensitive, confident example of how an industrial design, for all the dictates of the manufacturing process that informed it, can retain the human touch of the designer.

The Air-chair is stackable, lightweight, weatherproof and comparatively cheap to make and buy. Its 'chairy' shape counteracts the patio plasticness of the material, rendering it suitable for any occasion, formal or informal, indoor or outdoor. This versatility has made it the chair for the new millennium. Morrison modestly said of it, 'I think we succeeded in delivering a combination of angles and curves that give a lot of comfort.'

Right: An Air-chair emerging from a gas-injecting polypropylene casting mould. Below: A design sketch showing the clean form of Jasper Morrison's chair.

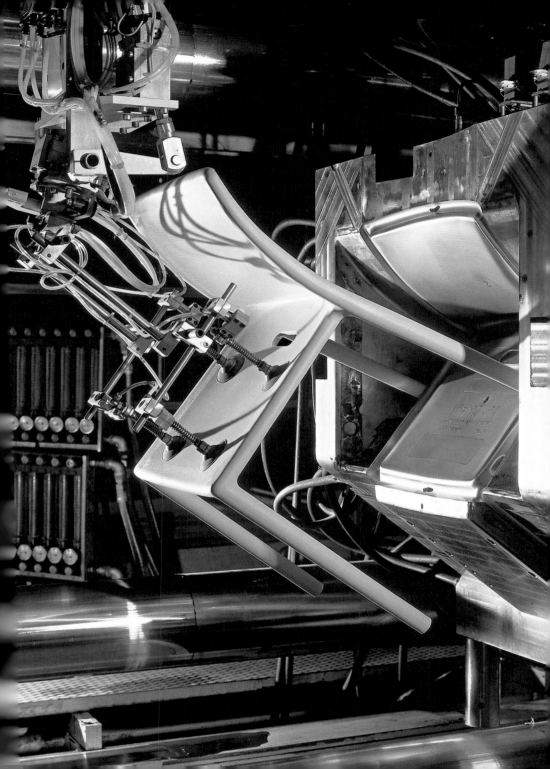

TREE TRUNK BENCH

Jurgen Bey

In today's high-tech, slick-shape world, where the eye is constantly distracted by the ceaseless, kaleidoscopic evolution of design, the Tree Trunk bench has the power to stop us in our tracks. Those who just don't get it may despair at its irreverent dismissal of the pursuit of design perfection. Those who approve of it will smile at its playful collaged composition and knowing irony.

The Rotterdam-based Dutch designer Jurgen Bey (1965–) has been described as someone who uses design as a way of telling stories – stories that critique and analyse our unthinking assumptions about the world around us. Among his best-known designs are the pieces that make up Vacuum Bag furniture (2004), in which he created comfortable seating out of dust and air pumped from a domestic vacuum cleaner – a manoeuvre that questions the hierarchies of what we consider useful and useless.

The tale that is being told in the Tree Trunk bench is about the highly complicated, processed and pondered objects with which we are constantly bombarded. The bench takes us several steps back to technological basics: an unrefined log is rendered purposeful with a definable function once a traditional chair back has been embedded within it.

The Tree Trunk bench is seating for the imagination – forcing us to think about its former incarnation as a tree and the intellectual journey that has transfigured it into a domestic object.

Right: The Tree Trunk bench challenges traditional chair design and materials with engaging wit.

SAMOURAÏ

2002
Ronan and Erwan
Bouroullec

Modern life seems to crave adaptability and versatility. Even the humblest of homes has to play host to a multiplicity of functions, habits and rituals, and furniture design, to be worthy of its name, must respond to an array of changing needs.

In the Samouraï, the French design duo Ronan (1971–) and Erwan (1976–) Bouroullec developed a chair that combines the lightness and portability of a conventional dining-room chair with the embracing comfort of an upholstered armchair. It is constructed out of three pieces of dense polyurethane foam wrapped around a stainless-steel base, and can be as easily assembled as disassembled and stored away.

The Bouroullec brothers took their inspiration from medieval suits of armour and named their chair after the Samurai, the Japanese military caste. It is a name that suggests not only the construction and protective role of the chair, but also its pared-down Japanist aesthetic. The Samouraï's combination of multifunctional design with a retro-inflected utilitarianism says a lot about our contemporary need for order and practicality, both in the public sphere and in the private, domestic one.

Right: The robust comfort of the Bouroullecs' chair, together with its innovative armour-like construction, suggested its naming after the medieval Japanese military caste.

CHAIR_ONE

2003
Konstantin Grcic

What will the chair of the future look like? Will it look as strange and disconcerting as Chair_One, the creation of the German designer Konstantin Grcic (1965–)?

Admittedly, Grcic developed the whole One series of die-cast aluminium furniture for Magis with the intention of producing something that was *deliberately* out of the ordinary, that would purposely and purposefully break the mould. Grcic constructed Chair_One 'like a football – a collection of small, flat planes assembled at angles to create a three-dimensional form'. The result is a cage-cum-cup in which the sitter can nestle like a bird in its nest.

The use of die-cast aluminium was a new technique for both designer and manufacturer, and is another reminder of how new technology is so often the driving force behind new design. (Turn back to the beginning of this book and you will see how the Thonet Side chair No. 14 was brought about by the innovation of steam-bent wood.)

However, much of the urgency to use new techniques to express modernity has passed. After more than a century of experimentation and innovation, reinvention and reinterpretation, the industrial aesthetic is the established norm. The slate is now cleaner than ever before for the designer to have freedom in which to exercise his or her creativity and self-expression.

Right: The web of die-cast aluminium rods in Konstantin Grcic's Chair_One is influenced by the structure of a leather football. Below: The seat can be mixed and matched with different bases.

INDEX

PICTURE CREDITS

CREDITS

First published in 2009
by Conran Octopus Ltd
a part of Octopus Publishing
Group, 2–4 Heron Quays
London E14 4JP
www.octopusbooks.co.uk

An Hachette Livre UK
Company
www.hachettelivre.co.uk

Distributed in the United
States and Canada by
Octopus Books USA, c/o
Hachette Book Group USA,
237 Park Avenue, New York,
NY 10017 USA

British Library Cataloguing-
in-Publication Data.
A catalogue record for
this book is available
from the British Library.

Text written by:
Michael Czerwinski

Publisher:
Lorraine Dickey
Consultant Editor:
Deyan Sudjic
Managing Editor:
Sybella Marlow
Editor:
Robert Anderson

Art Director:
Jonathan Christie
Design:
Untitled
Picture Researcher:
Anne-Marie Hoines

Production Manager:
Katherine Hockley
Production Controller:
Pauline Le Navenec

ISBN: 978 1 84091 504 2
Printed in China